MW01626990

The most AMAZING WOMEN of all time!

For Kids!

written by

Matilda Dibb

illustrated by Sam Cumbers

Are you ready to embark on an exciting adventure and meet the most amazing women of all time?

Each one of them has a unique story that will fill you with awe, excitement, and inspiration.

In this book, you'll read about women who broke barriers, stood up for what they believed in, and changed the world in incredible ways. These women come from different backgrounds, countries, and time periods, but they all have something in common: they were brave, determined, and followed their dreams, no matter what obstacles stood in their way.

Imagine flying high in the sky like Amelia Earhart, the first woman to fly solo across the Atlantic Ocean. Picture yourself leading a movement for justice like Rosa Parks, whose courageous act of defiance helped spark the civil rights movement. Think about using your voice to fight for equality, just like Malala Yousafzai, who stood up for girls' right to education despite the dangers she faced.

You'll also discover the stories of scientists like Marie Curie, who made groundbreaking discoveries, and artists like Frida Kahlo, who expressed their unique visions through their art. From athletes who broke world records to writers who changed the way we see the world, each of these women shows us that with passion and perseverance, anything is possible.

As you read about these incredible women, remember that you have the potential to do amazing things too. The world needs your unique talents, ideas, and dreams. So, get comfy, grab a snack, and dive into these stories. Let them inspire you to dream big, believe in yourself, and know that you can make a difference.

Are you ready to be inspired? Let's turn the page and start this incredible journey together.

The adventure begins now!

TABLE OF CONTENTS

GRETA THUNBERG

Taking a day off school and starting a global movement sounds crazy, right? That's exactly what Greta Thunberg did, becoming one of the most influential and inspiring young women of our time.

Greta Thunberg was born in 2003 in Stockholm, Sweden. From a young age, she was deeply concerned about climate change and the impact it was having on the world. She learned about the science behind it and couldn't understand why more wasn't being done to protect the Earth. Greta decided that she needed to take action.

In 2018, when she was just 15 years old, Greta began her climate activism by skipping school to protest outside the Swedish Parliament. She held up a sign that read, "School Strike for Climate," demanding stronger action from her government to combat climate change. At first, she protested alone, but her message quickly spread. Inspired by her courage, students from around the world joined her, leading to the creation of the "Fridays for Future" movement.

Greta's straightforward and powerful speeches have captivated audiences worldwide. She speaks passionately about the need for immediate action to address climate change and holds world leaders accountable for their inaction. One of her most famous speeches was at the United Nations Climate Action Summit in 2019, where she boldly declared, "How dare you!" challenging leaders to take responsibility for the future.

Despite facing criticism and challenges, Greta remains steadfast in her mission. She has inspired millions of people to care about the environment and take steps to reduce their carbon footprint. Her activism has led to greater awareness and urgency regarding climate change.

Greta Thunberg's story teaches us that no matter how young you are, you can make a significant impact on the world. She shows that with passion, determination, and a fearless spirit, anyone can be a force for change. Greta encourages us all to take care of our planet and fight for a better future.

Coco Chanel

Creating a style so timeless that people still love it a hundred years later is a remarkable achievement. That's what Coco Chanel did, revolutionizing the fashion world with her innovative designs and bold ideas.

Coco Chanel was born Gabrielle Bonheur Chanel in 1883 in France. She had a tough childhood. After her mother died, Coco was sent to an orphanage, where she learned to sew. Little did she know that this skill would one day change her life and the fashion industry forever.

Coco started her career by designing hats, which became very popular. In 1910, she opened her first boutique in Paris. But Coco didn't stop at hats; she wanted to change how women dressed. At that time, women's fashion was very elaborate and uncomfortable, with tight corsets and heavy fabrics. Coco had a different vision.

She believed that fashion should be comfortable and stylish. She introduced simple, elegant designs made from lightweight fabrics. One of her most famous creations was the little black dress, which became a symbol of elegance and simplicity. Coco also popularized the use of jersey fabric, which was previously only used for men's underwear. Her designs were revolutionary because they gave women freedom of movement and a modern, chic look.

Coco Chanel didn't just change clothing; she also made a big impact with her perfumes. In 1921, she launched Chanel No. 5, which became one of the most famous and best-selling perfumes in the world. It was unique because it was the first perfume to use a blend of scents, creating a complex and luxurious fragrance.

Coco Chanel's story teaches us about creativity, determination, and the power of believing in your vision. She showed that with hard work and bold ideas, you can change the world and leave a lasting legacy. Coco Chanel's innovative spirit continues to inspire fashion lovers everywhere to this day.

OPRAH WINFREY

Using your fame to help millions of people is not something that every celebrity does. But Oprah Winfrey did just that. She went from a challenging childhood to becoming one of the most influential women in the world!

Oprah was born in 1954 in a small town in Mississippi, USA. She had a tough upbringing, living in poverty and facing many hardships. Despite these challenges, Oprah was a bright and determined girl. She loved to read and was an excellent student, which helped her earn a scholarship to college.

Oprah's big break came when she moved to Chicago to host a morning talk show. Her warm personality and ability to connect with people made the show a huge success. In 1986, it was renamed "The Oprah Winfrey Show," and it quickly became the highest-rated talk show in television history. Oprah's show wasn't just about entertainment; she tackled important issues, shared inspiring stories, and interviewed famous guests, all while encouraging her audience to live their best lives.

Oprah didn't stop at just being a talk show host. She created her own production company, Harpo Productions, and later launched the Oprah Winfrey Network (OWN). Her business success made her one of the richest women in the world, but she never forgot to give back. Oprah has donated millions to charities and established schools for girls in South Africa, believing that education can change lives.

One of Oprah's most famous projects is her book club, which has helped millions of people discover the joy of reading. Her recommendations have turned many books into bestsellers, and her influence continues to inspire readers around the world.

Oprah Winfrey's story teaches us about resilience, hard work, and the power of believing in yourself. She showed that no matter where you start in life, you can achieve great things with determination and kindness. Oprah's incredible journey inspires us all to dream big and make a difference in the world.

KATHERINE JOHNSON

Have you ever looked up at the night sky and dreamed about exploring space? Well, there's an incredible woman named Katherine Johnson who played a huge role in making space travel possible!

Katherine Johnson was born in 1918 in West Virginia, USA. From a young age, she loved numbers and was incredibly talented at math. By the time she was ten years old, she was already in high school! She went on to college at just 15 and graduated with highest honors in mathematics.

After college, Katherine became a teacher, but her love for math and science led her to NASA, the American space agency. At NASA, she worked as a "human computer," performing complex calculations that were vital for space missions. Back then, electronic computers were just starting to be used, so people like Katherine did the math by hand.

Katherine's work was crucial in the early days of space exploration. She calculated the flight paths for the first American astronauts. One of her most famous contributions was for John Glenn's orbital mission in 1962. John Glenn, an astronaut, trusted Katherine so much that he asked for her to personally verify the calculations before his flight. Thanks to her precise math, his mission was a great success.

Katherine didn't just stop at John Glenn's mission. She also worked on the Apollo 11 mission, the first manned mission to the moon! Her calculations helped ensure that astronauts Neil Armstrong and Buzz Aldrin could land safely on the moon and return to Earth.

Throughout her career, Katherine faced many challenges, including racial and gender discrimination. But her determination, brilliance, and passion for math helped her overcome these obstacles. She opened doors for women and people of color in science, technology, engineering, and mathematics (STEM).

Katherine Johnson is a true inspiration. She showed that with hard work, perseverance, and a love for learning, you can reach for the stars—literally! So next time you gaze at the stars, remember Katherine Johnson, the mathematician who helped make space travel possible.

SOIT N C
A RT VARE
401×79
Suadgh ganrk ads oulh.mid
Med ae'T gotomm souchels
Elgla somy. raticha
Suces biron hews bon
coicoramd
anostes uued nde,
ounay mountalios.

Have you ever imagined what it would be like to be a queen?

Cleopatra, one of the most famous women in history, was the Queen of Egypt over 2,000 years ago. Her story is full of adventure, bravery, and cleverness.

Cleopatra was born in 69 BCE into a royal family. She became queen when she was just 18 years old! Unlike many queens before her, Cleopatra was determined to rule Egypt not just in name but with real power. She was very smart and could speak many languages, which helped her communicate with different people and leaders.

One of the things that made Cleopatra so remarkable was her intelligence. She wasn't just beautiful; she was also very wise and educated. She loved learning and surrounded herself with scholars. Cleopatra used her knowledge to make Egypt stronger and richer. She understood the importance of trade and built strong relationships with powerful leaders like Julius Caesar and Mark Antony from Rome.

Cleopatra's life was filled with dramatic moments. When her throne was threatened, she didn't give up. She even once rolled herself up in a carpet to sneak into a palace and meet Julius Caesar, who helped her regain her throne. Her bold actions showed that she was willing to do whatever it took to protect her kingdom.

Cleopatra and Mark Antony fell in love, and together they formed a powerful alliance. However, their enemies in Rome saw them as a threat. Despite their best efforts, Cleopatra and Antony's forces were defeated. Cleopatra was never captured however, showing her strong will and determination even in her final moments.

Cleopatra's story teaches us about the power of intelligence, bravery, and determination. She was a queen who didn't just sit on a throne but actively worked to make her kingdom a better place. Cleopatra's legacy lives on, reminding us that amazing women can shape history and inspire generations to come.

ELIZABETH I

Talking about queens, imagine being a queen at a time when many people thought women couldn't be strong leaders. Elizabeth I, the Queen of England, proved them all wrong. Her reign, which lasted from 1558 to 1603, is known as the Elizabethan Era and is considered one of the greatest periods in English history.

Elizabeth I was born in 1533 to King Henry VIII and Anne Boleyn. Her early life was full of challenges. After losing her mother, she was declared illegitimate. Despite these hardships, Elizabeth was very smart and loved to learn. She studied subjects like history, languages, and politics, which prepared her for the future.

When Elizabeth became queen at the age of 25, England was facing many problems. There were religious conflicts between Catholics and Protestants, and the country was at risk of being invaded by powerful enemies like Spain. Elizabeth had to be clever and strong to keep her kingdom safe.

One of her most famous achievements was defeating the Spanish Armada in 1588. Spain sent a massive fleet of ships to invade England, but Elizabeth's navy, with their smaller and faster ships, managed to outmaneuver and defeat them. This victory made Elizabeth a hero and strengthened England's position in the world.

Elizabeth I was known for her intelligence and wise decisions. She surrounded herself with trusted advisors and listened to their advice, but she always made the final decisions. She never married, saying she was married to her country.

Under Elizabeth's rule, the arts flourished. This era saw the rise of famous playwrights like William Shakespeare. The Elizabethan Era was a time of exploration and discovery, with adventurers like Sir Francis Drake sailing around the world.

Elizabeth I's reign showed that women could be powerful, wise, and successful leaders, and her legacy continues to inspire people today.

BENAZIR BHUTTO

Have you ever dreamed of making a big difference in the world? Benazir Bhutto did just that by becoming the first woman to lead a Muslim-majority country, Pakistan. Her life story is full of courage, determination, and a strong desire to help her people.

Benazir Bhutto was born in 1953 in Karachi, Pakistan, into a powerful political family. Her father, Zulfikar Ali Bhutto, was a former Prime Minister of Pakistan. Benazir was very smart and loved to learn. She went to some of the best schools in the world, including Harvard University and the University of Oxford.

When she returned to Pakistan, she faced many challenges. Her father was overthrown, and Benazir was put under house arrest. Despite these hardships, she didn't give up. She took over the leadership of her father's political party, the Pakistan Peoples Party (PPP), and continued to fight for democracy and the rights of her people.

In 1988, Benazir Bhutto made history by becoming the Prime Minister of Pakistan, the first woman ever to lead a Muslim-majority country. She was only 35 years old! As Prime Minister, she worked to improve the lives of the poor, increase women's rights, and bring modern technology to Pakistan. She focused on education, health care, and economic reforms.

Benazir's journey wasn't easy. She faced opposition and was removed from office twice, but she remained determined to serve her country. She was a symbol of hope and resilience for many women around the world.

Sadly, Benazir Bhutto's life was cut short in 2007 while campaigning. Despite the tragic loss, her legacy lives on. She showed that with bravery, intelligence, and a commitment to justice, you can break barriers and inspire millions.

Benazir Bhutto's story teaches us about the power of perseverance and the importance of standing up for what you believe in. She proved that women can be strong and effective leaders, no matter the challenges they face.

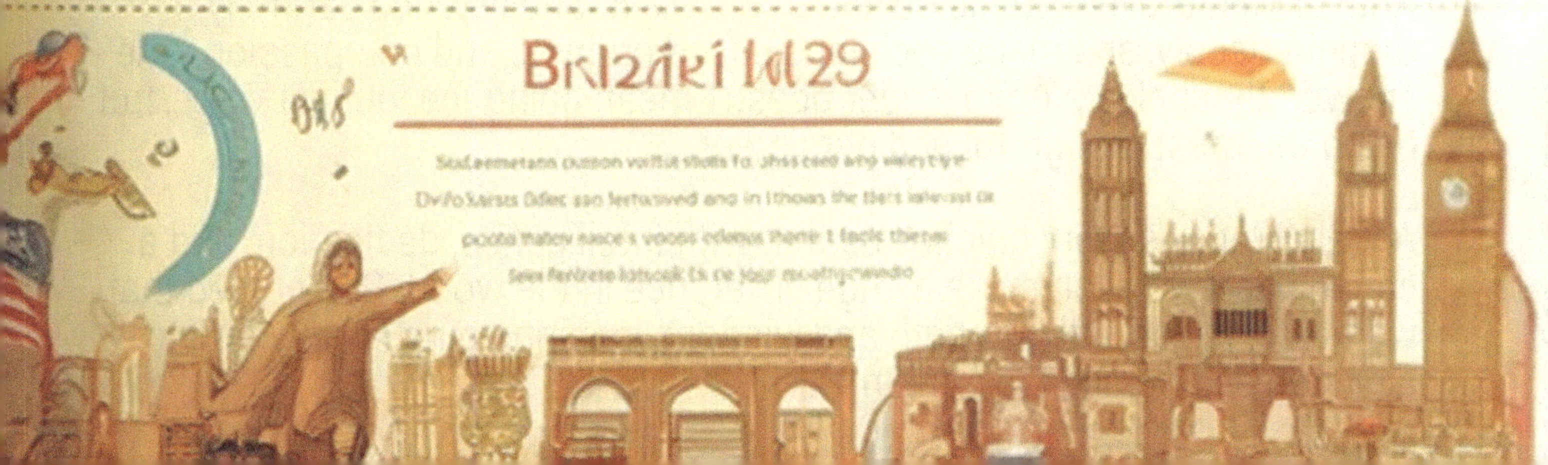

ANGELA MERKEL

Imagine being in charge of one of the world's most powerful countries! Angela Merkel did just that, serving as the Chancellor of Germany for 16 years and becoming one of the world's most influential women.

Angela Merkel was born in 1954 in Hamburg, Germany, but grew up in East Germany. She was very smart and loved science, especially physics. She studied hard and became a scientist, earning a doctorate in quantum chemistry. Angela's love for learning and her scientific mind helped her solve complex problems later in her career.

In 1989, something amazing happened: the Berlin Wall, which had divided East and West Germany, fell. This event changed Angela's life. She decided to enter politics to help shape the future of a reunited Germany. She joined a political party called the Christian Democratic Union (CDU) and quickly rose through the ranks because of her intelligence, hard work, and dedication.

In 2005, Angela Merkel became the first female Chancellor of Germany. As Chancellor, she faced many challenges, including economic crises and global issues. But she was known for her calm and steady leadership. She was often called "Mutti," which means "Mom" in German, because she cared deeply about the people of Germany.

One of her greatest achievements was helping to lead Europe through the financial crisis that began in 2008. She worked tirelessly to keep the European Union strong and united. Angela also focused on important issues like climate change, promoting renewable energy, and welcoming refugees during difficult times.

Angela Merkel's leadership style was different. She listened carefully, thought deeply, and made decisions based on facts and compassion. She showed that being a good leader doesn't mean being the loudest voice, but being the most thoughtful and persistent.

Angela Merkel's story teaches us that with intelligence, dedication, and a caring heart, you can make a huge difference in the world. She proved that women can lead with strength and wisdom, inspiring girls everywhere to aim high and pursue their dreams.

Imagine painting your dreams, your feelings, and your life's biggest adventures on a canvas. That's what Frida Kahlo did, and she's one of the most amazing women of all time!

Frida was born in Mexico in 1907. She had a big personality and loved bright colors, flowers, and animals. But life wasn't always easy for Frida. When she was a child, she got very sick with a disease called polio, which made one of her legs weaker than the other. Later, she was in a bus accident that caused her a lot of pain for the rest of her life.

Even though she faced many challenges, Frida found a special way to express herself: through painting. She often painted self-portraits, which are pictures of herself. Frida said she painted herself because she knew herself best. Her paintings show her emotions, her pain, and her love for her country.

Frida's art is full of bright, bold colors and lots of symbols. She painted animals like monkeys and birds, beautiful Mexican landscapes, and even herself with roots growing into the ground, showing how connected she felt to her homeland. Each painting tells a story, like a window into her heart and mind.

Besides being a talented artist, Frida was also very brave. She wasn't afraid to be different and to stand up for what she believed in. She wore traditional Mexican clothing with colorful skirts and embroidered blouses, celebrating her culture. Frida also spoke up for women's rights and equality.

Frida Kahlo's art and life remind us that it's okay to be different, to feel deeply, and to show the world who we truly are. She turned her struggles into beautiful art that still inspires people today. So, the next time you pick up a paintbrush, think of Frida and let your heart guide your creativity!

MAYA ANGELOU

Have you ever heard a story so powerful it changed the way you see the world? That's what Maya Angelou did with her words. She was a writer, poet, and activist who used her voice to inspire and uplift people all over the world.

Maya was born in 1928 in Missouri, USA. Her childhood was full of ups and downs. She faced many tough times, including being separated from her parents and experiencing racial discrimination. Despite these challenges, Maya found comfort in books and stories, which sparked her love for reading and writing.

When she was just a young girl, something very sad happened to Maya, and she stopped speaking for almost five years. But during this silent period, she listened carefully to the world around her and learned so much. Eventually, with the help of a kind teacher, she found her voice again and began to speak and sing.

Maya wrote many books, but one of the most famous is her autobiography, "I Know Why the Caged Bird Sings." This book tells the story of her early life and how she overcame adversity with courage and hope. Her writing is powerful because it is honest and full of emotion.

Not only was Maya a brilliant writer, but she also fought for civil rights. She worked alongside famous leaders like Martin Luther King Jr. and Malcolm X to help make the world a fairer place. She believed in equality and used her voice to speak out against injustice.

Maya's poems and books are celebrated for their beauty and strength. One of her famous poems, "Still I Rise," is all about overcoming challenges and standing tall no matter what. She showed that no matter how hard life gets, you can always rise above and be strong.

Maya Angelou's life reminds us to be brave, to use our voices for good, and to never give up. She turned her struggles into stories that inspire millions, teaching us that we can all rise and make a difference in the world.

MAYA ANGELOU

Have you ever looked at a building and thought it was so amazing it looked like a work of art? That's how people feel when they see the incredible buildings designed by Zaha Hadid. She was one of the most brilliant architects in the world and made her mark by designing unique and futuristic buildings.

Zaha Hadid was born in 1950 in Baghdad, Iraq. From a young age, she loved math and art, and she was always curious about how things were made. This curiosity led her to study architecture in London, where she dreamed of designing buildings that were different from anything anyone had ever seen.

Zaha became famous for her bold, modern designs. Her buildings often have smooth, flowing shapes that make them look like they're moving, even though they're made of solid materials like concrete and steel. People call her the "Queen of Curves" because she loved to use curved lines and unusual shapes in her work.

One of her most famous buildings is the Heydar Aliyev Center in Azerbaijan. This building looks like it's made from a giant, graceful wave of white steel and glass. It's stunning to look at and shows how Zaha could turn her imaginative ideas into real-life structures.

But Zaha's journey wasn't easy. Architecture is a field where there weren't many women, and she often faced challenges and people who didn't believe in her. However, she never gave up. She worked hard, believed in her vision, and became the first woman to win the prestigious Pritzker Architecture Prize, which is like winning an Oscar for architects!

Zaha Hadid's story shows us the power of imagination and perseverance. She turned her dreams into reality and changed the world of architecture forever. She teaches us that no matter where we come from or what obstacles we face, we can build a bright future with creativity and determination. So, the next time you see an amazing building, think of Zaha and remember that with hard work and creativity, you can shape the world too!

Imagine a world covered in bright, colorful polka dots. That's what the art of Yayoi Kusama feels like! Yayoi Kusama is a world-famous artist from Japan known for her unique and eye-catching creations filled with dots, bold colors, and mesmerizing patterns.

Yayoi was born in 1929 in Matsumoto, Japan. Even as a little girl, she loved drawing and painting. She started creating art when she was just 10 years old! Yayoi had a big imagination and often dreamed of making art that would cover entire rooms, creating magical spaces where people could feel like they were in another world.

In her twenties, Yayoi moved to New York City to follow her dream of becoming an artist. She worked very hard and faced many challenges, but she never gave up. Yayoi started creating large, colorful paintings covered in dots. These dots became her signature style, and she called them "infinity nets." They represented her feelings and thoughts, creating a sense of endless space and beauty.

One of the most famous things Yayoi creates is her "Infinity Mirror Rooms." These are special rooms filled with mirrors and lights that make it look like the patterns go on forever. When you step inside, it feels like you're floating in a magical, infinite universe of colors and dots.

Yayoi's art is not just about beauty; it's also about expressing her feelings. She has spoken about using art to cope with difficult emotions and experiences, turning her struggles into something beautiful and inspiring.

Today, Yayoi Kusama's work is celebrated all over the world. People of all ages visit museums to see her dazzling installations and colorful paintings. She teaches us that creativity has no limits and that even the wildest dreams can come true if you believe in yourself and keep working hard. So, the next time you see a polka dot, think of Yayoi Kusama and remember that art can make the world a brighter, more joyful place!

JOAN OF ARC

Imagine a young girl leading an entire army into battle! That's exactly what Joan of Arc did, becoming one of the most famous heroines in history.

Joan of Arc was born in 1412 in a small village in France. She was a peasant girl who didn't go to school but was very devout and deeply religious. At the age of 13, Joan began to hear voices that she believed were from saints telling her to help save France, which was suffering from a long war with England called the Hundred Years' War.

When Joan was 17, she felt a strong calling to take action. She convinced a local lord to take her to see the prince of France, later known as King Charles VII. Despite her young age and lack of military training, Joan's passion and conviction convinced Charles to let her lead an army to lift the siege of Orléans, a city under attack by the English.

Dressed in armor and carrying a banner, Joan inspired the French troops with her bravery and determination. She led them to several important victories, turning the tide of the war in favor of the French. People saw her as a symbol of hope and divine guidance.

Unfortunately, Joan's success also made her enemies. She was captured by the English and put on trial for charges like witchcraft and heresy. Even though she was just a teenager, Joan stood firm in her beliefs and refused to deny her visions. She was found guilty and tragically her life ended when she was only 19 years old.

Joan of Arc's courage and faith made her a martyr and a saint. Today, she is remembered as a national hero of France and a symbol of bravery and conviction. Her story teaches us that no matter how young or seemingly powerless we are, we can stand up for what we believe in and make a difference.

Joan showed that with courage and belief, even a simple girl can change the course of history.

HARRIET TUBMAN

Risking your life to help others find freedom is not something many people would do, but it is exactly what Harriet Tubman is famous for. She became one of the most courageous and amazing women in history because of her bravery and dedication.

Harriet Tubman was born around 1822 in Maryland, USA. She was born into slavery, which meant she had no freedom and had to work very hard from a young age. Life was incredibly tough, but Harriet was strong and determined. She dreamed of being free.

When Harriet was about 27 years old, she decided to escape from slavery. She bravely traveled over 90 miles to reach Pennsylvania, a state where slavery was illegal. The journey was dangerous, and Harriet had to be very careful to avoid being caught. But she made it! Harriet was finally free, but she didn't stop there.

Harriet wanted to help others escape slavery too. She became a "conductor" on the Underground Railroad, which was a secret network of safe houses and routes that helped enslaved people escape to free states and Canada. Harriet made about 13 missions back to the South and guided around 70 people to freedom, including her own family.

Harriet Tubman was incredibly brave and clever. She used the stars to navigate, and she traveled at night to avoid detection. She never lost a single person on her missions. People called her "Moses" because she led so many to freedom, just like Moses in the Bible.

During the American Civil War, Harriet worked as a nurse, cook, and even a spy for the Union Army. She continued to fight for freedom and justice her entire life.

Harriet Tubman's story teaches us about the power of bravery, determination, and kindness. She showed that one person can make a huge difference, no matter how difficult the circumstances. Harriet's legacy inspires us to stand up for what is right and to help others whenever we can. She proved that with courage and compassion, we can change the world.

HARRIET TUBMAN

MALALA YOUSAFZAI

Standing up for what you believe in is an admirable trait. Imagine doing it when it's dangerous?! Malala Yousafzai did just that and became a global symbol of bravery and the fight for girls' education.

Malala was born in 1997 in the Swat Valley of Pakistan. From a young age, she loved learning and dreamed of becoming a doctor. Her father, who ran a school, encouraged her education and inspired her to speak out about the importance of learning. But not everyone in her region believed that girls should go to school.

When Malala was just 11 years old, the Taliban, a group that opposed girls' education, took control of her valley. They banned girls from attending school and destroyed many schools. Malala refused to be silenced. She began writing a blog for the BBC under a pseudonym, sharing her experiences and advocating for girls' rights to education.

As Malala's voice grew louder, she gained international attention. However, her activism made her a target. In 2012, when Malala was only 15, a Taliban gunman boarded her school bus and attacked her. The world was shocked, but Malala survived the ordeal. Instead of being silenced, she became even more determined to fight for education.

After recovering, Malala continued her activism with even more strength. She and her father founded the Malala Fund, an organization dedicated to ensuring girls around the world have access to 12 years of free, safe, and quality education. In 2014, at just 17 years old, Malala became the youngest-ever Nobel Peace Prize laureate, recognized for her courageous efforts.

Malala's story teaches us about the power of education and the importance of standing up for what is right. She showed that even a young girl can make a huge difference in the world. Malala's courage and dedication inspire us all to value our education and fight for the rights of others.

MARIE CURIE

Marie Curie was an amazing scientist who made incredible discoveries that changed the world. Born in 1867 in Warsaw, Poland, her real name was Maria Skłodowska. From a young age, Marie loved learning and was especially interested in science.

Marie was super smart, but back then, it was really hard for women to get a good education. However, she didn't let that stop her! She moved to Paris, France, to study at a famous university called the Sorbonne. There, she met Pierre Curie, who was also a brilliant scientist. They got married and started working together on some groundbreaking research.

Marie and Pierre were curious about something called radioactivity, which is a special kind of energy that comes from certain elements. They discovered two new elements: polonium, named after Marie's homeland, and radium. Their work was so important that in 1903, Marie and Pierre, along with another scientist, won the Nobel Prize in Physics. Marie was the first woman to ever win a Nobel Prize!

But that's not all. In 1906, Marie became the first woman to teach at the Sorbonne and went on to win a second Nobel Prize in Chemistry in 1911 for her discovery of radium and polonium. This made her the first person ever to win two Nobel Prizes in different scientific fields!

Marie Curie's discoveries have had a huge impact on science and medicine. Her work with radium led to the development of X-ray machines, which are used in hospitals all over the world. Despite facing many challenges, Marie's dedication and passion for science never wavered.

Marie Curie is remembered as one of the most amazing women in history, a true pioneer who opened the doors of science for women everywhere. She showed us that with hard work and determination, we can achieve amazing things. So, the next time you hear about X-rays or scientific discoveries, remember the incredible Marie Curie!

ADA LOVELACE

Have you ever wondered how your tablet works? It's all because of computer programmers like Ada Lovelace who make the magic happen inside of your machine. Ada was a super-smart lady who lived in the 1800s. She loved math and science and was great at solving puzzles. She was born in London, England, and her mom made sure she learned all about numbers and logic.

From a young age, Ada showed a remarkable talent for numbers and logic. When she was a teenager, she met Charles Babbage, who was building a super cool machine called the Analytical Engine. It was like an early version of a computer. Ada was fascinated by this machine and started thinking about how it could do more than just simple math. She wrote notes and even created the first computer program! That's why she's known as the world's first programmer.

Ada's ideas were way ahead of her time. She imagined that computers could do amazing things like create music, make art, and even play games. Isn't that awesome? But life wasn't always easy for Ada. Being a woman in science back then was tough. Many people didn't believe that women could be good at math and science. But Ada didn't let that stop her. She kept working hard and proved them wrong.

One of Ada's most exciting ideas was that computers could follow a series of instructions, or what we call a program, to perform tasks. She even wrote an algorithm for the Analytical Engine to compute Bernoulli numbers, making her the first computer programmer in history!

Today, we celebrate Ada Lovelace as a pioneer in computer science. She showed us that with imagination and determination, we can achieve incredible things. So, the next time you use a computer, remember Ada Lovelace, the amazing lady who saw the future of technology. She's a fantastic example of how curiosity and hard work can lead to groundbreaking discoveries!

ROSALIND FRANKLIN

What makes you you?

The answer lies in something called DNA, which is like a blueprint for building every part of your body. And we have Rosalind Franklin to thank for helping us understand it!

Rosalind Franklin was born in London, England, in 1920. From a young age, she loved learning about science and solving puzzles. She studied very hard and became a scientist, focusing on something called X-ray crystallography. This might sound complicated, but it's just a way to take pictures of tiny things, like the molecules that make up our bodies.

One of the most important things Rosalind studied was DNA. DNA is like a set of instructions inside every living thing that tells it how to grow and function. Rosalind used her special skills to take a super clear picture of DNA. This picture, known as "Photo 51," showed the world that DNA has a special shape called a double helix. Imagine a twisted ladder – that's what a double helix looks like!

Rosalind's photo and her research were crucial. They helped other scientists, like James Watson and Francis Crick, to understand the structure of DNA. This discovery has been called one of the most important scientific breakthroughs ever because it helps us understand genetics, heredity, and even how to fight diseases.

Unfortunately, Rosalind didn't get the recognition she deserved during her lifetime. She passed away in 1958, and it was only later that people truly appreciated her vital contributions. Today, Rosalind Franklin is celebrated as a trailblazer who played a key role in one of the greatest scientific discoveries.

So, whenever you learn about DNA in school, remember Rosalind Franklin, the brilliant scientist whose hard work and dedication helped unlock the secrets of life itself. She showed that with curiosity, determination, and a love for science, you can achieve amazing things and change the world!

SHERYL SANDBERG

Have you ever thought about what it takes to lead one of the biggest companies in the world? Sheryl Sandberg did just that and became an inspiration for women everywhere by encouraging them to pursue their dreams and leadership roles.

Sheryl Sandberg was born in 1969 in Washington, D.C., USA. She was a bright and hardworking student who loved learning new things. After high school, Sheryl went to Harvard University, where she earned a degree in economics and later an MBA from Harvard Business School. Her education laid the foundation for her future success.

Sheryl started her career working for the U.S. government and then moved to Silicon Valley, the heart of the tech industry. She worked at Google, where she helped grow the company's advertising business. But her biggest opportunity came in 2008 when she joined Facebook as its Chief Operating Officer (COO). At Facebook, Sheryl played a crucial role in turning the social media platform into a profitable business, helping it grow into one of the world's most influential companies.

Beyond her work at Facebook, Sheryl is passionate about empowering women to achieve their goals. In 2013, she wrote a bestselling book called "Lean In: Women, Work, and the Will to Lead." The book encourages women to be more assertive in their careers, seek leadership roles, and support each other. It sparked a global movement, with "Lean In" circles forming worldwide where women gather to share advice and encouragement.

Sheryl's story is not just about business success. She has faced personal challenges, including the sudden loss of her husband, and she has openly shared her experiences to help others cope with their own struggles. Her resilience and dedication to helping others make her a role model for many.

Sheryl Sandberg's journey teaches us that with hard work, education, and a strong belief in ourselves, we can overcome obstacles and achieve great things. She inspires girls to dream big, lead confidently, and support each other in reaching their full potential.

Rosa Parks

One action that changed the world.

That's what Rosa Parks did when she refused to give up her seat on a bus, becoming a hero in the fight for civil rights.

Rosa Parks was born in 1913 in Alabama, USA. Growing up in the South, she experienced the harsh realities of segregation, where African Americans were treated unfairly and had to use separate facilities from white people. Despite these challenges, Rosa was determined and hardworking. She finished high school at a time when very few African Americans had that opportunity.

On December 1, 1955, Rosa did something incredibly brave. She was riding a bus in Montgomery, Alabama, and when the bus became crowded, the driver told Rosa and other African American passengers to give up their seats for white passengers. Rosa refused. She knew this was unfair and decided to stand up for her rights by staying seated. Her act of defiance led to her arrest, but it also sparked a much larger movement.

Rosa's courage inspired the Montgomery Bus Boycott, where African Americans refused to ride the buses for over a year to protest segregation. The boycott was led by Dr. Martin Luther King Jr. and brought national attention to the civil rights movement. Eventually, the Supreme Court ruled that segregation on public buses was unconstitutional, a huge victory for civil rights.

Rosa Parks didn't stop fighting for justice after the boycott. She continued to work for equality throughout her life, becoming an important symbol of courage and determination.

Rosa Parks' story teaches us that one person's brave actions can make a big difference. She showed that standing up for what is right, even when it's difficult, can lead to positive change. Rosa inspires us all to be courageous and fight for justice, reminding us that everyone has the power to make the world a better place.

RICSA PARK

POCAHONTAS

Have you ever heard the story of Pocahontas? She was a real person, not just a character in a movie, and her life was full of courage and kindness.

Pocahontas was born around 1596 as the daughter of Powhatan, the powerful chief of a network of tribes in what is now Virginia, USA. Her real name was Amonute, and she had the nickname Matoaka. The name Pocahontas, which means "playful one," was a childhood nickname.

When Pocahontas was about 11 years old, English settlers arrived and built a fort at Jamestown. Relations between the Native Americans and the settlers were often tense, but Pocahontas played a key role in fostering peace. According to one story, she saved the life of Captain John Smith, an English leader, when her father was about to execute him. While historians debate the details of this event, it's clear that Pocahontas was important in the relationship between her people and the settlers.

Pocahontas continued to help the settlers by bringing them food and messages. In 1613, she was captured by the English during a conflict with her tribe. During her captivity, she converted to Christianity and took the name Rebecca. She also met and married John Rolfe, an English tobacco planter. This marriage helped establish a period of peace between the settlers and the Native Americans.

In 1616, Pocahontas traveled to England with her husband and son. She was presented to English society in a very unkind way. This was an attempt to encourage investment in the Jamestown settlement. Pocahontas was well received and met many important people, including King James I. Sadly, she became ill and died in 1617 at the young age of about 21.

Pocahontas' story teaches us about bravery, compassion, and the importance of understanding and respecting different cultures. She showed that even one person can make a significant impact by acting as a bridge between worlds. Her legacy inspires us to work towards peace and mutual respect in our own lives.

ANNE FRANK

Having to hide from danger while finding the strength to write about your experiences must be extremely hard. That's what Anne Frank did, and her diary has touched the hearts of millions around the world.

Anne Frank was born on June 12, 1929, in Frankfurt, Germany. She was a happy, outgoing girl who loved to write stories and dreamed of becoming a famous writer. But when she was just a little girl, the world around her changed drastically. Adolf Hitler and the Nazis came to power in Germany, and they didn't like Jewish people, like Anne and her family.

To escape the increasing danger, Anne's family moved to the Netherlands. However, when the Nazis invaded the Netherlands, life became dangerous again. In 1942, when Anne was 13, her family went into hiding in a secret annex behind her father's business. For two years, they lived in this small, hidden space with another family and a dentist, always in fear of being discovered.

During her time in hiding, Anne wrote in her diary, which she named "Kitty." She wrote about her thoughts, feelings, and the daily challenges of living in hiding. Despite the fear and hardships, Anne's writing was filled with hope and dreams for the future. She believed in the goodness of people, even in the darkest times.

Sadly, in 1944, the secret annex was discovered, and Anne and her family were arrested. Anne was sent to a concentration camp, where she died in 1945 at the age of 15. After the war, her father, Otto Frank, was the only family member who survived. He found Anne's diary and decided to publish it, so the world could hear her story.

Anne Frank's diary, "The Diary of a Young Girl," has been translated into many languages and read by millions. Her story teaches us about the horrors of war, but also about the strength of the human spirit. Anne's courage, hope, and ability to find beauty in the world, even in the toughest times, continue to inspire people everywhere.

FLORENCE NIGHTINGALE

Have you ever wanted to help others and make a big difference in the world? Florence Nightingale did just that. She became a pioneer in nursing and saved countless lives with her dedication and compassion.

Florence Nightingale was born on May 12, 1820, in Florence, Italy. From a young age, she felt a strong desire to help people. Even though it was unusual for women of her time to work in medicine, Florence knew that she wanted to be a nurse. Her family was wealthy and didn't understand why she wanted to work in hospitals, but Florence was determined.

In the 1850s, a war broke out called the Crimean War. Florence heard about the terrible conditions for wounded soldiers and knew she had to help. She traveled to the war zone with a team of nurses she had trained. When they arrived, they found overcrowded hospitals with dirty conditions. Many soldiers were dying from infections more than from their injuries.

Florence worked tirelessly to improve the conditions. She cleaned the hospitals, ensured there was enough food, and provided proper care for the soldiers. She would walk the halls at night with a lamp, checking on the patients. The soldiers began to call her "The Lady with the Lamp" because of this. Her efforts greatly reduced the death rate and showed how important good nursing care is.

After the war, Florence continued her work in nursing. She wrote books and established the first professional nursing school, the Nightingale Training School for Nurses in London. Her work laid the foundation for modern nursing and inspired many people to follow in her footsteps.

Florence Nightingale's story teaches us about compassion, determination, and the impact one person can make. She showed that caring for others and improving health care can save lives and change the world. Florence's legacy continues to inspire nurses and caregivers everywhere, reminding us that with dedication and kindness, we can make a difference.

AMELIA EARHART

Have you ever dreamed of flying high above the clouds, exploring new places, and breaking records? That's exactly what Amelia Earhart did, becoming one of the most famous aviators in history with her courage and adventurous spirit.

Amelia Earhart was born on July 24, 1897, in Atchison, Kansas. From a young age, she was curious and loved to explore. She wasn't afraid to break the rules and often played rough and tumble games that were unusual for girls at that time. Her adventurous spirit continued to grow as she got older.

Amelia's passion for flying began when she took her first plane ride in 1920. She was immediately hooked and knew she wanted to become a pilot. At a time when very few women were in aviation, Amelia worked hard to make her dream come true. She took flying lessons, saved money to buy her own plane, and eventually earned her pilot's license.

In 1928, Amelia made headlines by becoming the first woman to fly across the Atlantic Ocean as a passenger. But she wasn't satisfied with just being a passenger. In 1932, she became the first woman to fly solo across the Atlantic, facing dangerous weather and mechanical problems but landing safely in Ireland. This incredible achievement made her an international hero and proved that women could do anything they set their minds to.

Amelia didn't stop there. She continued to set records and inspire people around the world with her daring flights. She even attempted to fly around the world in 1937. Sadly, during this journey, her plane disappeared over the Pacific Ocean, and despite extensive searches, she was never found. Her bravery and determination, however, continue to inspire.

Amelia Earhart's story teaches us about courage, perseverance, and the power of following your dreams. She showed that with hard work and a fearless heart, you can break barriers and achieve greatness. Amelia's legacy encourages girls everywhere to reach for the stars and explore the endless possibilities in their own lives.

PRINCESS DIANA

Princess Diana became a beloved figure known for her kindness, compassion, and dedication to helping those in need.

Princess Diana was born on July 1, 1961, in England. She became Lady Diana Spencer after her father inherited the title of Earl Spencer. In 1981, Diana married Prince Charles, making her Princess Diana. Her wedding was watched by millions around the world, and she quickly became a global icon.

But Diana was much more than a princess in a fairy tale. She used her position to shine a light on important issues and help those who were often ignored. She was known for her genuine kindness and ability to connect with people from all walks of life. Diana visited hospitals, homeless shelters, and orphanages, always offering a comforting touch and a warm smile.

One of Diana's most significant contributions was her work with people affected by viruses. At a time when there was much fear and misunderstanding about some diseases, Diana showed incredible bravery by shaking hands and hugging patients. Her actions helped reduce the stigma around that particular disease and changed how people viewed those with the illness.

Diana was also passionate about raising awareness for landmines, which cause injuries and death long after wars have ended. She visited countries affected by landmines, walking through minefields to draw attention to the issue. Her efforts played a crucial role in the international campaign to ban landmines.

Princess Diana's life was tragically cut short in a car accident in 1997, but her legacy lives on. She is remembered as "The People's Princess" because of her ability to touch hearts and make a real difference.

Princess Diana's story teaches us about the power of compassion and the importance of using our voices to help others. She showed that kindness and empathy can change the world, inspiring us to make a positive impact in our own communities.

BILLIE JEAN KING

Billie Jean King is one of the greatest tennis players in history and also a powerful advocate for gender equality.

She was born on November 22, 1943, in Long Beach, California. Billie discovered her love for tennis at a young age and quickly showed incredible talent. With determination and hard work, she became a top player, winning her first major championship at just 17 years old.

Throughout her career, Billie Jean won 39 Grand Slam titles, including 12 in singles, making her one of the most successful tennis players ever. But her achievements on the court were only part of her amazing story. She noticed that female athletes were not treated equally to their male counterparts. Women earned much less prize money and received less respect and recognition.

Billie Jean decided to fight for change. In 1973, she took on Bobby Riggs, a former men's tennis champion who claimed that women were inferior athletes. Their match, known as the "Battle of the Sexes," was watched by millions. Billie Jean's victory was not just a win for herself but a powerful statement for women everywhere, proving that women could compete at the highest levels.

Billie Jean continued to advocate for women's rights and equality in sports. She co-founded the Women's Tennis Association (WTA), which gave female tennis players a stronger voice and better opportunities. She also started the Women's Sports Foundation to support girls and women in all sports.

Billie Jean King's story teaches us about courage, determination, and the importance of standing up for what is right. She showed that you can be a champion both on and off the court. Her legacy inspires girls to pursue their passions and fight for equality, reminding us that everyone deserves the chance to succeed.

MICHELLE OBAMA

Being a role model for millions of people and using your voice to make a positive impact on the world. That's what Michelle Obama did as the First Lady of the United States, inspiring countless people with her intelligence, kindness, and dedication to important causes.

Michelle Obama was born on January 17, 1964, in Chicago, Illinois. Growing up, she was a bright student who loved to learn. Her parents encouraged her to work hard and dream big. Michelle went on to attend Princeton University and Harvard Law School, becoming a successful lawyer.

In 1992, Michelle married Barack Obama, who would later become the 44th President of the United States. When Barack was elected president in 2008, Michelle became the First Lady. In this role, she used her platform to advocate for several important causes that she cared deeply about.

One of Michelle's major initiatives was the "Let's Move!" campaign, which aimed to combat childhood obesity and encourage kids to lead healthier lives. She promoted exercise, better nutrition, and healthy eating habits, inspiring children and families across the country to make positive changes.

Michelle also launched the "Reach Higher" initiative, encouraging young people to pursue higher education and career training. She believed that every child deserved a chance to succeed and worked tirelessly to support students in achieving their dreams.

Another important cause for Michelle was supporting military families and veterans. She co-founded the "Joining Forces" initiative to provide resources and support for those who serve and their families.

Michelle Obama's story teaches us about the power of education, hard work, and using our voices to help others. She showed that with determination and compassion, we can make a difference in the world. Michelle's legacy continues to inspire girls everywhere to dream big, stay healthy, and work hard to achieve their goals.

bigs
Bte
Ddk y yo dack
ire gastaphan.

DOROTHY HODGKIN

Have you ever wondered how scientists discover the tiny secrets of nature? Dorothy Hodgkin did just that, becoming one of the most amazing women in science. Her groundbreaking work helped us understand the structures of important molecules, changing the world of chemistry and medicine.

Dorothy Hodgkin was born on May 12, 1910, in Cairo, Egypt, but grew up in England. From a young age, she was fascinated by science, especially chemistry. She loved to explore how things were made up at the tiniest level. Her curiosity and passion led her to study chemistry at the University of Oxford.

Dorothy specialized in a field called X-ray crystallography, a technique that allows scientists to see the three-dimensional structures of molecules. This might sound complicated, but it's like taking a super detailed photograph of something so tiny that it can't be seen with regular microscopes. Using this method, Dorothy made some incredible discoveries.

One of her most famous achievements was determining the structure of penicillin, an important antibiotic that saves countless lives. Before her work, scientists didn't fully understand how penicillin worked at the molecular level. Dorothy's discovery helped improve the production of antibiotics, making them more effective.

But she didn't stop there. Dorothy also mapped the structure of vitamin B12, which is vital for our health, and insulin, which is crucial for people with diabetes. Her work on insulin has helped millions of people manage their diabetes more effectively.

In 1964, Dorothy Hodgkin was awarded the Nobel Prize in Chemistry for her outstanding contributions. She remains the only British woman to have won this prestigious award in chemistry.

Dorothy Hodgkin's story teaches us about the power of curiosity, perseverance, and the importance of following your passion. She showed that women can achieve great things in science and make discoveries that change the world. Her legacy inspires girls everywhere to explore the wonders of science and pursue their dreams with determination and creativity.

Imagine running so fast that you end up being the best in the world. Wilma Rudolph did just that, becoming an Olympic champion and an inspiration to many with her incredible speed and determination.

Wilma Rudolph was born on June 23, 1940, in Tennessee, USA. She was the 20th of 22 children in her family. When she was very young, Wilma faced many health challenges. She had polio, a disease that caused her leg to become weak and twisted. Doctors said she might never walk again without a brace.

But Wilma was determined and never gave up. With her family's support and her own hard work, she learned to walk without her brace by the time she was nine years old. By 12, she could run and play like other kids. Her determination didn't stop there; she decided to become a runner.

In high school, Wilma joined the track team and quickly became a star. She was so fast that she earned a spot on the U.S. Olympic team at just 16 years old, competing in the 1956 Olympics. But her greatest achievements came in the 1960 Olympics in Rome, where she made history.

Wilma won three gold medals in the 100 meters, 200 meters, and 4x100 meter relay, making her the first American woman to win three gold medals in track and field at a single Olympics. Her incredible speed earned her the title "The Fastest Woman in the World."

Wilma's success went beyond the track. She became a symbol of hope and inspiration, especially for African Americans and women, showing that with hard work and determination, you can overcome any obstacle. After retiring from running, she worked as a teacher and coach, helping young athletes achieve their dreams.

Wilma Rudolph's story teaches us about resilience, determination, and the power of never giving up. She showed that no matter how tough the challenges, you can achieve greatness with hard work and a strong spirit. Wilma's legacy inspires girls everywhere to chase their dreams and believe in themselves.

118

Aung San Suu Kyi

Aung San Suu Kyi stood for what she believed in, even when it was dangerous to do so. That saw her become a symbol of hope and courage in her country, Myanmar, as she fought for democracy and human rights.

Aung San Suu Kyi was born on June 19, 1945, in Yangon, Myanmar (then called Burma). Her father, Aung San, was a national hero who helped lead Burma to independence from British rule, but she sadly lost him when she was only two years old. Her mother continued to inspire her with stories of bravery and dedication to their country.

Suu Kyi was a brilliant student and went on to study in India and at the University of Oxford in England. She got married and had two sons, living a peaceful life abroad. But in 1988, she returned to Myanmar to take care of her sick mother. She noticed her country was in turmoil. The military government was harsh, and many people were suffering.

Inspired by her father's legacy, Suu Kyi decided to stand up against the oppressive regime. She became the leader of the National League for Democracy (NLD) and began advocating for peaceful change and democracy. Her speeches and peaceful protests attracted many supporters but also made her a target for the military government.

In 1989, Suu Kyi was placed under house arrest. She spent 15 of the next 21 years in detention, separated from her family. Despite the hardships, she never gave up. Her commitment to non-violence and her refusal to leave Myanmar, even when she had the chance, inspired people around the world.

In 1991, Suu Kyi was awarded the Nobel Peace Prize for her non-violent struggle for democracy and human rights. In 2010, she was finally released from house arrest and continued her efforts to bring democracy to Myanmar.

Aung San Suu Kyi's story teaches us about bravery, perseverance, and the power of peaceful resistance. She showed that one person's dedication to justice can inspire a nation and bring about change. Her legacy encourages girls everywhere to stand up for what is right and to believe in the power of peaceful actions.

SOJOURNER TRUTH

Speaking up for what's right is incredibly important. Sojourner Truth did just that, becoming one of the most powerful voices for freedom and equality in the 1800s.

Sojourner Truth was born around 1797 in New York State. Her birth name was Isabella Baumfree, and she was born into slavery. Life as a slave was incredibly harsh, and she faced many hardships. Despite these challenges, Isabella grew up strong and determined.

In 1826, Isabella made a brave decision: she escaped from slavery with her infant daughter. She found refuge with a kind Quaker family who bought her freedom. After gaining her freedom, she changed her name to Sojourner Truth because she felt called to travel (sojourn) and spread the truth about slavery and injustice.

Sojourner Truth was a remarkable speaker. Even though she never learned to read or write, she used her powerful voice to fight for the abolition of slavery and for women's rights. She traveled across the United States, giving speeches about the need for equality and justice. Her most famous speech, "Ain't I a Woman?", was delivered in 1851 at a women's rights convention. In it, she spoke about the strength and capabilities of women, challenging the idea that women were weaker or less capable than men.

Sojourner Truth also worked to help freed slaves after the Civil War. She dedicated her life to improving the lives of others, showing incredible bravery and compassion. Her efforts helped pave the way for future generations to fight for equal rights.

Sojourner Truth's story teaches us about courage, resilience, and the power of using your voice to stand up for what is right. She showed that even in the face of great difficulties, one person can make a significant difference. Her legacy inspires girls everywhere to speak out against injustice and to believe in their own strength and worth.

GERTRUDE STEIN

Your words and art can come together to create something magical. Just look at what Gertrude Stein achieved in her life. She became a groundbreaking writer and a central figure in the world of modern art and literature.

Gertrude Stein was born on February 3, 1874, in Allegheny, Pennsylvania. When she was a young girl, her family moved to Europe, where she developed a love for art and literature. Gertrude was a bright student and went on to study at Radcliffe College, part of Harvard University, where she began to explore her passion for writing.

In 1903, Gertrude moved to Paris, France, with her brother Leo. Their home quickly became a gathering place for some of the most famous artists and writers of the time, including Pablo Picasso, Henri Matisse, and Ernest Hemingway. These gatherings were called "salons," where people shared ideas, discussed their work, and inspired each other. Gertrude's salon was one of the most famous in Paris.

Gertrude Stein's writing was different from anything people had seen before. She played with words and sentences, creating a unique style that broke the traditional rules of writing. Her most famous work, "The Autobiography of Alice B. Toklas," is actually about her own life, told through the eyes of her lifelong partner, Alice. Another well-known work, "Tender Buttons," is a collection of poems that describe everyday objects in new and imaginative ways.

Although her writing was sometimes difficult to understand, Gertrude Stein's innovative style had a big impact on literature and art. She encouraged others to see the world differently and to express themselves in new ways.

Gertrude Stein's story teaches us about creativity, courage, and the importance of following your own path. She showed that it's okay to be different and to explore new ideas. Her legacy inspires girls to embrace their creativity, think outside the box, and celebrate the beauty of art and words.

BETTY FRIEDAN

Have you ever wondered what it would be like to change the world with your ideas? That's what Betty Friedan did. She became a powerful voice for women's rights and helped spark a movement that changed society.

Betty Friedan was born on February 4, 1921, in Peoria, Illinois. She was a curious and intelligent girl who loved to read and write. Betty went to college and studied psychology, a field that explores how people think and feel. After college, she worked as a journalist, writing articles about important social issues.

In the 1950s, many women in the United States felt unfulfilled and unhappy. Society expected them to be perfect housewives and mothers, but many women wanted more out of life. Betty Friedan noticed this and decided to investigate why so many women were feeling this way. She sent out a survey to her former college classmates and discovered that many of them felt the same dissatisfaction.

Betty wrote a book about her findings called "The Feminine Mystique," published in 1963. The book became a bestseller and started a national conversation about women's rights and their roles in society. It helped many women realize that they weren't alone in their feelings and that they deserved to pursue their own dreams and ambitions.

In 1966, Betty co-founded the National Organization for Women (NOW), an organization dedicated to fighting for gender equality. She worked tirelessly to promote equal opportunities for women in the workplace, education, and other areas of life. Her efforts helped pave the way for important changes in laws and attitudes about women's rights.

Betty Friedan's story teaches us about the power of speaking out and fighting for what is right. She showed that one person's ideas can inspire millions and bring about real change. Her legacy encourages girls everywhere to stand up for their rights, pursue their passions, and believe in their ability to make a difference in the world.

Valentina Tereshkova

When you look at the stars and the moon at night, do you ever wonder what it would be like to fly up there?

Valentina Tereshkova did just that! She became the first woman to travel into space, inspiring millions with her bravery and adventurous spirit.

Valentina Tereshkova was born on March 6, 1937, in a small village in Russia. Her family worked in a textile factory, and Valentina helped out from a young age. She was an adventurous girl who loved parachuting, a hobby that would later help her achieve her dreams.

In 1961, Yuri Gagarin became the first human to travel into space, and the Soviet Union wanted to continue making history. They decided to send a woman into space and began searching for the right candidate. Valentina's experience with parachuting caught their attention, and she was selected from more than 400 applicants to join the space program.

After rigorous training, Valentina was ready for her mission. On June 16, 1963, she launched into space aboard Vostok 6. For nearly three days, Valentina orbited the Earth 48 times, conducting experiments and taking photographs. She communicated with ground control and even kept a detailed flight log. Her journey proved that women could endure the challenges of space travel just as well as men.

Valentina's historic flight made her a global hero. She received numerous awards and honors for her achievements. But she didn't stop there. After her spaceflight, she continued her education, earned a doctorate in engineering, and became a prominent figure in politics, working to promote science and technology.

Valentina Tereshkova's story teaches us about courage, determination, and the power of breaking barriers. She showed that no dream is too big and that with hard work and bravery, you can achieve anything. Valentina's legacy inspires girls everywhere to reach for the stars and pursue their own dreams fearlessly.

GLORIA STEINEM

Gloria Steinem spent her life fighting for fairness, and in doing so she became a leading voice for women's rights and equality.

Gloria was born on March 25, 1934, in Toledo, Ohio. As a young girl, she loved to read and learn about the world. Her mother faced many challenges, and Gloria saw firsthand the struggles that women often experienced. This inspired her to work towards making the world a better place for women.

After college, Gloria became a journalist. She noticed that women's voices and issues were often ignored in the media. Determined to make a change, she started writing articles that highlighted the importance of women's rights.

In 1971, Gloria co-founded a magazine called Ms. Magazine, which was one of the first magazines to talk about women's rights and issues important to women. The magazine gave women a platform to share their stories and ideas, inspiring many to join the fight for equality.

Gloria didn't just write about change; she also took action. She helped start the National Women's Political Caucus, which encourages women to run for political office, and worked tirelessly to pass laws that protect women's rights. She traveled across the country, giving speeches and organizing rallies to raise awareness about gender equality.

Gloria Steinem's story teaches us about the power of using our voices to stand up for what is right. She showed that one person can make a big difference by speaking out and fighting for fairness. Her dedication to equality and justice inspires girls everywhere to believe in themselves and work towards a world where everyone is treated equally.

Gloria Steinem's legacy encourages us to dream big, stand up for our rights, and support each other in making the world a better place for everyone.

ANNE MORROW LINDBERGH

Fying high in the sky and exploring the world is what Anne Morrow Lindbergh liked to do best! She was a famous aviator and writer who soared through the skies and inspired many with her courage and creativity.

Anne Morrow Lindbergh was born on June 22, 1906, in Englewood, New Jersey. She loved reading and writing from a young age, and she was also very curious about the world. Her life changed forever when she met Charles Lindbergh, the famous pilot who made the first solo nonstop flight across the Atlantic Ocean. They got married, and Anne's adventure began.

Anne didn't just support Charles; she became a pilot herself. She learned to fly and helped navigate during their long flights together. In 1930, she became the first American woman to earn a first-class glider pilot's license. Anne and Charles flew to many places around the world, breaking records and exploring new routes.

Anne loved writing about her experiences in the sky. She wrote several books, sharing her adventures and thoughts with the world. Her most famous book, "Gift from the Sea," is a collection of essays reflecting on life and relationships. It's still loved by many readers today.

But Anne's life wasn't just about flying. She faced many challenges and hardships. Despite these difficulties, she remained strong and continued to inspire others with her writing and bravery.

Anne Morrow Lindbergh's story teaches us about the power of adventure, resilience, and following our passions. She showed that girls can be brave pilots and thoughtful writers, exploring the world and sharing their stories. Anne's legacy encourages us to dream big, embrace our creativity, and never be afraid to take to the skies in pursuit of our dreams.

SIMONE DE BEAUVOIR

Have you ever wondered why it's important for everyone to have equal opportunities, no matter if they're a boy or a girl? Simone de Beauvoir thought a lot about this and became a famous writer and philosopher who fought for women's rights and equality.

Simone de Beauvoir was born on January 9, 1908, in Paris, France. She was a bright and curious girl who loved to read and learn. When she grew up, she went to university, which was quite rare for women at that time. She studied philosophy, which is the study of big ideas about life, knowledge, and existence.

Simone wanted to understand why women were often treated differently from men and why they didn't have the same opportunities. She wrote a very important book called "The Second Sex" in 1949. In this book, she explored how society views women and argued that women should have the same rights and opportunities as men. She famously wrote, "One is not born, but rather becomes, a woman," meaning that society teaches women to behave in certain ways.

Her book was groundbreaking and sparked conversations all over the world about gender equality. It encouraged many people to think about how women are treated and inspired the feminist movement, which fights for equal rights for women.

Simone was not just a thinker; she was also a doer. She worked with many groups to improve the lives of women and to support their rights. She believed that everyone should be free to pursue their dreams and live their lives without unfair limitations.

Simone de Beauvoir's story teaches us about the power of thinking deeply and standing up for what is right. She showed that through writing and activism, one person can make a big difference. Simone's legacy encourages girls to question unfairness, pursue education, and work towards a world where everyone is treated equally.

ELIZABETH BLACKWELL

Saving people's lives is one of the greatest things you can do. Elizabeth Blackwell did just that by becoming the first woman doctor in the United States. Her story is one of determination, courage, and breaking barriers.

Elizabeth Blackwell was born on February 3, 1821, in Bristol, England. When she was a young girl, her family moved to the United States. Elizabeth was very curious and loved learning about everything, especially science. Back then, people believed that only men could become doctors, but Elizabeth wanted to change that.

Elizabeth decided to apply to medical schools, but it wasn't easy. Many schools rejected her just because she was a woman. Finally, she was accepted into Geneva Medical College in New York. Some people thought it was a joke and didn't believe a woman could succeed in medical school. But Elizabeth was determined to prove them wrong.

She worked incredibly hard and faced many challenges, but she never gave up. In 1849, Elizabeth graduated at the top of her class, becoming the first woman in America to earn a medical degree. She showed everyone that women could be great doctors, too!

After becoming a doctor, Elizabeth wanted to help other women follow in her footsteps. She opened her own clinic in New York City, where she treated women and children who couldn't afford medical care. Later, she founded the New York Infirmary for Women and Children, which also served as a training facility for female doctors and nurses.

Elizabeth's dedication didn't stop there. She helped start the first medical college for women, providing them with the education and opportunities they needed to become doctors.

Elizabeth Blackwell's story teaches us about the power of perseverance and believing in ourselves. She showed that with hard work and determination, we can overcome obstacles and achieve our dreams. Elizabeth's legacy inspires girls everywhere to pursue their passions and make a positive impact on the world, no matter the challenges they face.

YOUR TURN TO SHINE!

You've just read about the incredible lives of nearly 40 of the most amazing women to ever live. Each of these women faced their own challenges and obstacles, yet they never gave up. They pursued their dreams, stood up for what they believed in, and made a huge impact on the world. Now, it's your turn to shine!

Remember, just like Elizabeth Blackwell, who became the first woman doctor, and Valentina Tereshkova, who soared into space, you too can achieve anything you set your mind to. The stories of these inspiring women show us that with hard work, determination, and a strong belief in yourself, you can overcome any challenge.

Think about Malala Yousafzai, who fought for girls' education even when it was dangerous, or Rosa Parks, who stood up for what was right and sparked a movement for civil rights. These women started with small steps that led to big changes. You can make a difference too, no matter how small your actions may seem at first.

Dream big! If you want to be a scientist, an artist, an athlete, a leader, or anything else, know that it's possible. The world needs your unique talents, ideas, and passion. You have the power to change the world in your own special way.

Remember, it's okay to face setbacks and obstacles. Every great woman you read about in this book faced challenges, but they never gave up. They kept going, and so can you. Surround yourself with supportive friends and family, keep learning, and stay curious.

You are the future. You are capable of achieving great things and making the world a better place. Believe in yourself, follow your passions, and always strive to be the best version of yourself. The world is waiting for you to make your mark.

So go out there, dream big, and change the world! The next chapter is yours to write.

Thank you for sharing this adventure with us!

If you enjoyed the journey, we'd love to hear your thoughts.

Your reviews are like little hugs for our book. Please leave a sprinkle of stars and a dash of kind words on your favorite platform.

It really helps independent authors like myself!

Happy reading, and thank you for being a part of our story!

Made in the USA
Las Vegas, NV
08 July 2024